More Precious than Pearls

The Mother's Blessing and God's Favour towards Women

More Precious than Pearls: The Mother's Blessing and God's Favour towards Women

© 2016 Anne Hamilton and Natalie Tensen

Published by Armour Books
P. O. Box 492, Corinda QLD 4075, Australia
www.armourbooks.com

ISBN: 9781925380064

Cover Photo Credit: pressmaster (Canstock photos)

National Library of Australia Cataloguing-in-Publication entry

Creator:	Hamilton, Anne, 1954- author.
Title:	More precious than pearls : the mother's blessing and God's favour towards women / Anne Hamilton ; Natalie Tensen.
ISBN:	9781925380064 (paperback)
Subjects:	Women--Prayers and devotions.
	Women--Religious aspects.

Other Creators/Contributors: Tensen, Natalie, author.

Dewey Number: 242.643

More Precious than Pearls

The Mother's Blessing and God's Favour towards Women

Anne Hamilton
Natalie Tensen

Scripture quotations marked HCSB®, are taken from the Holman Christian Standard Bible®, Copyright © 1999, 2000, 2002, 2003, 2009 by Holman Bible Publishers. Used by permission. HCSB® is a federally registered trademark of Holman Bible Publishers.

Scripture quotations marked HNV are taken from the Hebrew Names Version of the Bible. Public domain.

Scripture quotations marked KJV are taken from the King James Version of the Bible. Public domain.

Scripture quotations marked NASB are taken from the New American Standard Bible®, Copyright © 1960, 1962, 1963, 1968, 1971, 1972, 1973, 1975, 1977, 1995 by The Lockman Foundation. Used by permission. (www.Lockman.org)

Scripture quotations marked NLT are taken from the Holy Bible, New Living Translation, copyright 1996, 2004. Used by permission of Tyndale House Publishers, Inc., Wheaton, Illinois 60189. All rights reserved.

Scripture quotations marked NIV are taken from the HOLY BIBLE, NEW INTERNATIONAL VERSION®. Copyright © 1973, 1978, 1984 Biblica. Used by permission of Zondervan. All rights reserved.

Scripture quotations marked NKJV are taken from the New King James Version. Copyright © 1982 by Thomas Nelson, Inc. Used by permission. All rights reserved.

Scripture quotations marked NRS are taken from New Revised Standard Version of the Bible, copyright 1952 [2nd edition, 1971] by the Division of Christian Education of the National Council of the Churches of Christ in the United States of America. Used by permission. All rights reserved.

Scripture quotations marked TPT are taken from The Passion Translation™, copyright © 2011. Used by permission of 5 Fold Media, LLC, Syracuse NY 13039, United States of America. All rights reserved.

Dedication

Dell Hamilton
Ann Elizabeth
with much love

Art credits:

Chapter 1 —Benjamin West: Portrait of Elizabeth Shewell West and Her Son Raphael; c. 1770

Chapter 2 —Museyushaya: Traditional Jewish Wedding Ceremony; Canstockphotos

Chapter 3 —Asta Lander: Comfort Angel; astalander.com.au

Chapter 4 —NeoCortex: Semitic Traditional Young Woman (1888); Dollarphotos

Chapter 5 —Robyn Kannan: New Beginnings; robynkannan.com

Chapter 6 —Kayleen Jensen: Kiss the King; facebook.com/kayleenjensenfinearts

Chapter 7 —Safina Stewart: Strong Communites 2 (2011); Traditional Country: Mabuiag Island, Torres Strait and Wuthathi Country, QLD; www.artbysafina.com.au

Endnotes —Robyn Kannan: The Gift; robynkannan.com

Prayer Credit

O'Hara, J., The Mustard Seed, Hesed Publications. Nambour: Queensland 2010

Contents

1	Woman and Mother: Armour-Giver	4
2	Woman and Mother: Armour-Bearer	13
3	Woman and Mother: Watchman	25
4	Woman and Mother: Cupbearer	34
5	Woman and Mother: Game-changer	44
6	Woman and Mother: Gatekeeper	53
7	Woman and Mother: Above Pearls	63
	Endnotes	73

Prologue

ON MY WAY TO WORK each morning I pass a huge roadside billboard. It has a royal purple background with just four fat white words. The dramatic lettering always draws my eye. 'Mum deserves the best.'

It's an ad for a nursing home.

It's simple but shrewd. And it implies so much with so few words: after all mum's years of sacrifice, it's time to repay her for all she's done.

It goes without saying mums are very special people. The typical mum has wiped messy bottoms for us as babies, band-aided scrapes as we've grown into toddlers, praised our kindergarten scribbles as she stuck them on the fridge, helped us with school homework, given us pocket money, taxied us through our teenage years.

She's usually been the one to buy the birthday and Christmas presents. Perhaps it came naturally to her because the most ancient sense of the word 'lady' is bread-giver or gift-giver.

Mum is the one who comforts, nurtures, protects.

And we tend to take her for granted. That's why the ad is so effective. It's not just about remembering mum's sacrifice, it's also about recalling how easy it is to forget all she's done.

Perhaps there's an aspect of culture in it all. People of the West don't have as high a view of mothers as do those of the East. The influence of society in the intellectual West even affects the way mothers are presented in the Bible. Their role tends to be glossed over and sidelined in translations and commentaries.

So, before we proceed to the Mother's Blessing at the end of each chapter, let's look at how God sees mothers. All too often women have such a low view of the feminine, we don't believe we have a genuine blessing to impart. Not having received a blessing from mum, we don't know where to start for our own children. So let's begin by looking at the Bible's real view of women. Be prepared for a surprise!

1
Woman and Mother: Armour-Giver

1
Woman and Mother: Armour-Giver

BEN'S MOTHER WAS OUT SHOPPING and he was home alone with his little sister Sally. So, as small boys do, he decided to entertain himself. He made up his mind to paint a portrait.

Finding some bottles of coloured ink, he set to work. Very soon stains were everywhere. A trail of smudges showed his progress around the room.

When his mother returned, she surveyed the mess in absolute silence. She said nothing until she spotted the portrait. 'Why, it's Sally!'

She kissed him.

'My mother's kiss made me a painter,' recalled Benjamin West in later years.

He was to go on to become one of the most celebrated artists of the eighteenth century.

A kiss is never *just* a kiss.

In Scripture, a kiss is also the means by which we are given armour. It's no coincidence that concealed within the armour of God, mentioned in Ephesians 6:13–18, are references to peace, faith, righteousness and truth. This combination of virtues alludes to the *kiss* of heaven and earth in Psalm 85:10–11.

It's also meant to be a subtle reminder that, in Hebrew, *to kiss* is identical to the word for *to put on armour*. Initially that might seem strange but, if you think for a moment, you'll see the depth of insight in it: a tender embrace gives us strength for the battles of each day. A hug tells us we're not alone when life is reduced to a fight. A kiss is the finest combat gear available when we need to be kitted out for daily warfare.

When we don't receive enough warm, wholesome cuddles as babies, we crave affection as we grow older. When we aren't held lovingly as toddlers, we grow up without armour to shield us from the world.

Touch is life-giving.

Rarely has this been more evident than when Isobel's grandson was born. She asked her friends to pray up a storm when her daughter-in-law Kate faced a premature delivery of twins. At just 26 weeks into the pregnancy, the chances of survival were greatly reduced. In fact, the older of the twins, Jamie, didn't begin breathing and was given just moments to live.

After twenty minutes, the doctors stopped their efforts to save him. 'I saw him gasp…' Kate insisted. But the doctors had given up.

Kate asked to hold Jamie's body and told her husband David to join her in embracing him. 'We had tried for years to have kids…' she said. 'I just wanted to cuddle him… We were trying to entice him to stay. We explained his name and that he had a twin that he had to look out for and how hard we tried to have him. He suddenly gasped... then he opened his eyes. He was breathing and grabbing Dave's finger.'

'If we had let the doctor walk out of the room with him, Jamie would have been dead.'

Touch is life-giving. After birth, skin-to-skin contact is widely recognised as a helpful welcome for babies to assist them in adapting to a new environment.[1]

After the fall of the dictator Nicolae Ceaușescu, orphanages all over Romania were charged with caring for abandoned babies. Many children sickened and died in these overcrowded institutions. However a few thrived. And these few had something really odd in common: they were the infants nearest the door. What preferential treatment were they receiving?

When the matter was examined, the only thing to come to light was that these were the babies most likely to receive a soft pat or a gentle caress from a nurse or cleaner as she entered or exited the room.

Just the sort of things mothers naturally give us.

We're designed for hugs.[2]

And when we're denied affectionate touch—a simple hug, a pat on the shoulder, a tousle of the hair—we come to yearn for signs of love and acceptance. The hollow inside us wants to be filled. Eventually we're led to gratify this need in the wrong way and the wrong places. We cling to those who give us acceptance or offer us approval and support—even when we know they're manipulating us for their own purposes.

God has many names. The first He ever revealed has strong, maternal overtones. Fourteen years after God had cut a blood covenant with Abram, He appeared to him to undertake a name covenant. He initiated this second covenant by announcing His name was 'El Shaddai'.

By the end of the name exchange, Abram had become Abraham, and Sarai, Sarah. The 'h' given to both of them came from God's own name. In Jewish understanding, *hei*, 'h', symbolises fruitfulness and pregnancy. In giving Abram an 'h' from His own name, God offered a divine promise their long-desired son would soon on the way. The waiting was almost over.

A new name restores us to the estate God has set aside as our inheritance. It ushers us into our destiny. When Sarai became Sarah, her years of barrenness were at an end. She was about to inherit the promise of a special child—one born of her own body.

The maternal overtones to this covenant didn't end with the 'h' of Abraham's and Sarah's new names. They're also apparent in God's proclamation of Himself as 'El Shaddai'. Normally this is translated *God Almighty* but it literally means: *God, the strong-breasted one*.

God told Abraham that He is the supreme nurturer. As children of Abraham, grafted into his family tree, God wants to draw us into the circle of His arms. He wants to cherish us, treasure us, and lavish His unmeasurable gifts upon us.

In his portrait, *The Return of the Prodigal Son*, Rembrandt painted the figure of the father bending over to the kneeling son as having one masculine hand and one more feminine hand. In this way, he imaged the paternal and maternal attributes of God. In the time of the prophets, God's protection was likened to the wings of an eagle. Sometimes He defended His people by hiding them in His shadow, sometimes by lifting them on His back. In the time of Jesus, when the eagle symbolised the brutal, subjugating armies of Rome, God's protection was likened instead to that of a mother hen with her chicks.

Both eagle and hen are true. Both lion and lamb.

Even if we've turned away from Him, God is ready to meet us where we are and bring us back. He yearns to sing a lullaby over us (Zephaniah 3:17) and quiet us with His love. His peace, security, solace and armour are all ready.

Just waiting.

Quiet your mind and raise your face for His armour-giving kiss.

Prayer for Myself:

Thank You, Lord of heaven, for revealing Yourself first of all in a name that speaks of motherly care. Nurture me so I can nurture others. Where I have not received nurture, fill the hollow that has been left by the lack.

Kiss me so that I am clothed in Your armour and grant me the ability to clothe others in armour too. Allow me to give and receive the gentle gifts of genuine smiles and wholesome hugs, butterfly kisses and tender caresses that speak to the world of Your name, El Shaddai.

Draw me into the circle of Your arms and let me rest there while I learn the song You are singing over me and come to attune myself to the desires of Your heart. Quiet me with Your love, cover me with the freshness of Your sweet, deep peace and allow me to claim the greatest and most cherished treasure of all—Yourself.

In the name of Jesus and through the power of El Shaddai, the God who comforts and nurtures.

Amen

Prayer for my Children:

Child, as a mother today, according to God's Word, I want you to know that you are special and unique in His eyes. I ask that you be seen by others today through heaven's eyes, a blessing to the world at this very moment in time.

As a mother today I want to bless you, from the very time of your conception; to this very minute. I bless each day that you have been on this earth. I bless your design and I welcome you as the gift that you are to the world, to your friends and family.

I ask for the 'shalom'—the abundant peace of God—to wash over you. Lord, would You pour in Your divine and perfect nurture. Beloved, I bless your spirit—calling you forth into life and into the destiny your heavenly Father has for you.

I bless you with heaven's peace. May it flow over you into the deepest parts of the heart, spirit and body. I ask El Shaddai to lift shame off your identity and ask Him to restore peace to the places where anxiety has taken root through unmet needs—El Shaddai would You draw out any trauma of rejection or abandonment. I ask instead that You pour in love, gentleness and compassion to my child's spirit and body; cleansing and washing away that which has been in its place.

El Shaddai, lift the shame off Your child that resulted from a feeling that it was necessary to perform to be accepted. That love was conditional and subject to criticism. I ask your forgiveness for those times. Where I could not nurture, or where there was a lack of comfort or availability—if you did not develop strong attachment—I ask El Shaddai to please restore comfort and security to your precious child.

In the name of Jesus and through the power of El Shaddai, the God who comforts and nurtures.

Amen

2
Woman and Mother: Armour-Bearer

2
Woman and Mother: Armour-Bearer

AN AMAZING DANCE, THE *HORA*, is performed at traditional Jewish weddings. The guests surround the bride and groom and lift them up on chairs. It's an exhilarating and sometimes white-knuckle terrifying moment for the couple as they sway above the heads of the guests. The groom has a small white cloth—he flings out one end for the bride to catch, linking the two of them together in the dance.

The action of lifting the couple on chairs is a symbolic reminder of what marriage is meant to be. The Hebrew word for *married*, 'nasu', comes from the word 'nasa", *to lift up*. The dance tells the couple that God's intention for marriage is that the partners lift each other up.

As those chairs teeter around the room with the bride and groom on top, the newly-weds are demonstrating what marriage should mean: mutual uplifting and upbuilding, supporting and raising up. They are to upbuild each other in love so that they can rise up to meet challenges together, surmount obstacles together, pull each other up when needed, be each other's support and climbing companion on the uphill journey of life.

Surprisingly—the *hora* dance is also symbolic of submitting. One of the Hebrew words for *submission* also comes from 'nasa", *to lift up*.[3]

In fact, this Hebrew word for *submission* is diametrically opposed in conception to its Greek counterpart, 'hupotasso'. While they both have military overtones, the Hebrew word has the sense of *lifting up* while the Greek has the sense of *being under* or *being put down.* Over time, with our reliance on the Greek nuances instead of the Hebrew, *submitted* has become partnered with *subdued.*

Paul clearly recognised the possibility of a misunderstanding when it comes to submission. He went to great pains to explain the mutuality of 'hupotasso' straight after he said to the Ephesian women: '*Wives, submit to your own husbands.*' (Ephesians 5:22 ESV)

Now these women had previously participated in the worship of Ephesian Artemis. When they'd turned to Christianity, together with their husbands, they'd burnt their scrolls of spellcraft and sorcery as well as with their objects of ritual magic. (Acts 19:19) They'd renounced their devotion to the goddess of the city. Yet, Paul's choice of the military word, 'hupotasso', suggests the remnants of a lingering loyalty in the women's thinking. The city's founders were the fabled Amazons—female warriors, renowned for despising both men and marriage.

Because of this background, Paul's selection of 'hupotasso' makes perfect sense. He was addressing women who had worshipped the way of the warrior. And he was telling them, using martial language, not to despise their male partners but to support them. To see marriage as a beautiful reflection of Christ's love for the church.

Submit is not the only possible translation of 'hupotasso'. *Support* is a valid alternative. Most translations overlook it however in favour of the traditional *submit* or *be subject to*.

Brian Simmons in The Passion Translation renders 'hupotasso' in Colossians 3:18 as *supportive and tenderly devoted.* In arriving at this translation, he uses both Greek and Aramaic texts to inform his version. However, preferring a rendering solely from the Aramaic when it comes to Ephesians 5:22, he gives us: '*…wives, this means being tenderly devoted to your husbands like you are tenderly devoted to our Lord.*'

That rendition draws up meaning from more than one ancient translation, giving us a more contextualised sense of Paul's thought. But it still lacks the military flavour of Paul's original words. So I prefer: '*Wives, lift up your husbands. Be their companions for battle.*'

Not 'battle companions' in an attacking sense. Rather in a defensive sense. In Hebrew thinking, submission is deeply tied to protection, covering, watching over and shielding. It's so integral to the idea of safeguarding and cherishing one another that the verse, '*Wives, submit to your husbands*' is not the only occasion Paul goes on from submission to talk first about love and then secondly about armour.

He does the same thing in Romans 13:1 HCSB when he says: '*Submit to the governing authorities.*' Back in Ephesians, he goes on to detail the component pieces of the armour of God, while in Romans he speaks of waking up to put on the armour of light.

This transition isn't coincidental.

Armour, as we've seen, is about a kiss. Submission in Scripture begins with a song and ends with a kiss. A divine kiss: the supernatural kiss of God that clothes us in invincible armour.

Embedded in the Hebrew idea of submission is a complex picture of a battle companion—a helper armed with initiative, courage and loyalty. Some believers want to reduce this image to that of a servile, obedient robot.

But a battle companion is never to be considered an unthinking automaton. In being called to *submit*, a wife is called to the role of a 'paraclete'. In a law court, the 'paraclete' was the person who stood beside you, advocating your case. On a battlefield, the 'paraclete' was your partner—the teammate who'd trained with you so that, in the thickest combat, you'd become a single fighting unit. You'd both manoeuvre so you could fight back to back, protecting each other. If one of you fell, it was the role of the paraclete to stand astride the wounded body of the other, fighting on and providing a covering shield. When the battle was over, your paraclete would carry you off the battlefield, comfort you and tend your wounds.

The Hebrew equivalent of the Greek word for *battle partner*, 'paraclete' was 'nasa' keliy', *armour-bearer*. The armour-bearer was the covenant companion, recognised as the *keeper of her partner's head*. When headship, under the curse of sin, is perverted into domination, the armour-bearer is restricted in her ability to perform her calling.

Instead of realising that Paul's admonition in Ephesians 5:22 is about *mutual* uplift, some husbands use it as a justification for aggression and control—even for despising women who do not submit. Ironically, a direction to women who lived in a culture with a long history of despising men has been turned on its head. Men have despised their partners by throwing out the context of Paul's direction to the Ephesian women not to despise theirs!

Throughout the world, domestic violence is rising sharply to unprecedented heights. In Australia, this was once an uncommon cause of death. However, at the present time, an average of nearly two women a week are killed by their partners. The church must bear considerable responsibility in this area. Paul's words have been so frequently taken out of context in the past that a culture of male domination grew up. In many areas today, it still exists—sometimes subtly, sometimes overtly.

To fight directly against it is to play its own game. I've had both male and female bosses and, frankly, the latter have been the worst tyrants. Perhaps it's because they're trying to prove something.

To destroy domination, we need to understand the biblical concept of submission and apply it to both marriage and government.

In being called to submit to God, we're called to lift Him up. He's not a repressive, oppressive or suppressive King. He calls us to be rulers with Him. As we lift Him up, He lifts us up. One word for *ruler* or *prince* is 'nasiy', derived from 'nasa". The Aramaic word for *wives* is 'nasiyn'.[4]

Paul's poetic thoughts when he wrote, '*Submit to the governing authorities*' combine two derivatives of the same root, 'nasiy' and 'nasa" to say: *lift up the rulers*. His poetic thoughts when he wrote '*Wives, submit to your husbands*,' combine similar words, 'nasiy' and 'nasa", to say: *wives, lift up*…

The implication in the first case: lift up the rulers of the people so that together you build a nation rising to greatness and drawing others to the holy uplifted Name of God. The implication in the second case: lift up your covenant partner so that together you can build a family who will mutually support each other and rise up to draw others to the holy uplifted Name of God.

Yes, there is a name of God that means *lifted up*. When God revealed Himself as Yahweh Nissi, it was at a desperate time in Israel's history. The title 'nissi' from 'nasa" means *lifted up*, however the name is usually translated as *the Lord my Banner*.

In Exodus 17, the fierce desert-dwelling Amalekites attacked the Israelites while they were wandering in the wilderness. Moses directed Joshua to lead the counter-attack as he went up a hill to pray to God. Picture how exhausted he must have been physically and emotionally: he'd just dealt with a million people (if you think I'm exaggerating, no—I'm underestimating) who'd been complaining bitterly about dying from lack of water. In a stressful ordeal, God had told him to strike a rock with his staff to let water flow.

One crisis gives way to another as the camp is attacked. Moses goes up the hill with that same staff and raises it skywards. And as his arms are stretched to heaven, the Israelites prevail. As soon as his hands start to droop, the Israelites lose. Aaron and Hur have to stand at his sides, lifting up his arms until such time as the Amalekites are totally defeated.

Yahweh Nissi refers to the God who covers us in battle as we lift up our hands in prayer and praise. It refers to working together as one team: Joshua couldn't do it alone. He couldn't fight the battle without divine help and that required Moses to keep calling on the name of the One who lifts up, carries His people in battle and bears them safely through the day of conflict. However Moses couldn't do it alone, either. He couldn't be a rallying point when he was dropping with fatigue. Consequently he was dependent on Aaron. And even Aaron couldn't do his bit alone: he needed help from Hur.

Joshua took the lesson of Yahweh Nissi—*the Lord my banner*—very much to heart. Many years later, in the middle of a similar battle against the Amorites,[5] he called on God for a miracle: he asked for the sun to stand still.

The word for *miracle*, 'nes', is also derived from 'nasa".

Isn't this incredible? When spouses mutually support each other, when parents mutually support their children, they become part of the name of God.

Miracles happen.

Prayer for Myself:

Lift me up, heavenly Father, so that I can lift You up. Bear me up on eagle's wings so that I can raise Your name higher. Raise Your banner of love over me so that I can raise a banner of love to honour Your Name.

Whenever I am tempted to despise men, like the Amazons of old, pull me up and give me the grace to repent. I repent of the times I have failed to honour my earthly father; my brothers in blood and in the Lord; my husband and my sons.

Lord, help me to be a wife who lifts up and a mother who lifts up. Help me to show You—Yahweh Nissi—to my husband, my children, my friends, and to strangers. Grant me a miracle of strength, patience, faith, endurance and love to be able to do the impossible. Lift my hands, O Lord, so my acts of motherhood praise You.

Thank You, Jesus, and thank You, Holy Spirit, for being the 'keeper of the head', my paraclete and battle companion, my armour-bearer and covenant defender. Praise You for Your faithfulness and Your willingness to shield me when I take refuge in You. Reveal to me those hiding places I have where I find comfort away from You and prompt me to always seek Your covering.

Father God, please kiss me so I will be clothed in Your armour. Help me to repair any holes or gaps in the armour You give me by showing me what I need to forgive, actions I need to repent of and habits I need to confess and put behind me. Gift me with divine balance so that I know that, even though You call me to be an armour-bearer, I should never get in Your way as the heavenly Armour-bearer. Grant me wisdom so that I can discern how to be a paraclete but never get in Your way as the heavenly Paraclete. Give me understanding so that I can be a covenant defender but still never get in your way as the heavenly Covenant Defender.

In the name of Jesus and through the power of Yahweh Nissi, the God who lifts us up and holds a banner of love over us.

Amen

Prayer for my Children:

Lord, over Your precious ones, I ask for the kiss of heaven—which is the armour of God—to cover them today. I ask You to surround these precious lives with Your protection and peace. Jesus, I ask You to shelter them under Your healing 'wings'—Your prayer shawl— wrapping them into Your prayers before the Father. Like a mother bird covering and giving warmth to her children, would You, God, cover them and shield them—especially as I pray for healing and restoration.

I ask You, Father, to lift off shame and any fear of being seen. As Your children's hearts open, would You give them the courage to be vulnerable; to be free to ask for what they need; to turn from being afraid; to no longer desire to be hidden.

Child, as a mother today, according to God's Word, I again want you to know that you are special and unique in God's eyes.

I ask that you be seen by others today through heaven's eyes—as a blessing to the world at this very moment in time. Like Esther, who was born and released by both grace and favour into a divine time in history, may you be released by the Lord to be one who stands for Justice and Mercy in your generation.

I release you today, child, to be hidden in Christ and to find your strength in Him alone. I send you to Him so He will arm you with strength and courage for the journey you are walking out today.

Heavenly Father, would You show your child how to connect with You and also how to drink from Your river—the river that flows from Your throne.

I bless you, child, with knowing this connection as your true source of peace and protection.

In the name of Jesus and through the power of Yahweh Nissi, the God who lifts us up and holds a banner of love over us.

> Amen

3
Woman and Mother: Watchman

3
Woman and Mother: Watchman

'Your beauty should not come from outward adornment, such as braided hair and the wearing of gold jewellery and fine clothes. Instead, it should be that of your inner self, the unfading beauty of a gentle and quiet spirit, which is of great worth in God's sight. For this is the way the holy women of the past who put their hope in God used to make themselves beautiful.'

1 Peter 3:3–5 NIV

THE HONOUR ACCORDED TO WOMEN in Scripture is often obscured by our tendency to uproot a verse and examine it outside of the ground in which it's planted.

Take, for instance, Peter's words about women's beauty. A casual reader of almost any English translation would see these verses as prohibiting beauty shops, hairdressers, jewellery and expensive clothes. And, over the centuries, that sort of ban is exactly what some religious people—both men and women—have insisted on. Such a literal interpretation can often make women feel like second-class citizens, relegated to long-haired dowdiness.

Ironically an exact rendering of these verses would command women never to wear anything at all! The fact is, modern translators invariably insert a qualifier like 'fine' in front of 'clothes'. They feel compelled to put in an adjective that's not in the original!

So, no hairdresser? Well, ok, I guess we could all go for the Rapunzel look.

No jewellery? I suppose there's some merit in that—it would mean that we don't cause other women to stumble through jealousy or a feeling they need to compete.

But *no clothes*? Aha, that explains why we need the Rapunzel look!

Facetious comments aside, it's all too easy to forget that translation *always* contains some aspect of interpretation. Modern translators have rightly looked behind the bare words and universally inserted an adjective so that it's clear Peter is not suggesting nudity.

It's a pity so many of them have only done it at this particular point and missed the subtle allusion just before it. Ancient echoes of gender-specific faithfulness reverberate across this passage, all keyed into the words 'gold jewellery'.

Some sixteen hundred years before Peter wrote this epistle, the people of Israel were camped around Mount Sinai. Moses was on the mountain, talking to God—and taking so long about it, the people got restless. Eventually, under pressure, Aaron told the men to ask everyone for gold—their wives, their sons, their daughters.

Melting down the valuable jewellery collected, Aaron supervised the creation of a golden calf. Moses, when he finally came down the mountain after forty days, was appalled. He threw down the sapphire tablets with the commandments engraved on them and they smashed.

Now it doesn't matter which English translation you consult (and I've personally looked at over sixty), there's absolutely no indication in even one of them that the women *didn't* participate in the creation of the golden calf.

However, the fact is: they had nothing to do with it. Hidden in the pronouns, according to Jewish rabbis, is the clear indication that Aaron did not receive any gold for the idol from the women.

Now, perhaps you're thinking that the mothers of Israel simply didn't want to part with all the lovely bling they'd been given by the Egyptians when they left. You'd be wrong. This was a matter of faithfulness. And that's made abundantly clear when later, at the time Moses asked for gifts of gold for the adornment of the Tabernacle, the women led the way.

Again, the fidelity of the women isn't obvious in any English translation.

Rabbi Yechiel Eckstein makes the comment that a crucial detail has been omitted from the following rendering: *'All who were willing, men and women alike, came and brought gold jewellery of all kinds: brooches, earrings, rings and ornaments. They all presented their gold as a wave offering to the Lord.'* (Exodus 35:22 NIV)

He points out that, in Hebrew, the verse more literally reads: *'The men came on the heels of the women and brought gold jewellery of all kinds…'*[6]

Yes, the same women who had refused to surrender their gold ornaments for the golden calf were first in line to offer them for God's Tabernacle. They also handed over the brass mirrors they'd been given by the Egyptian women to be reforged into the vast laver, the washing basin, for the Tabernacle entrance:

That's not all! According to various Jewish commentators, they were the first to agree to the covenant of the Law.[7] God treated women differently as a consequence: He instructed Moses to speak to them with gentle encouragement and to men with stern admonition.[8]

Perhaps this is why Peter's exhortation in his epistle is full of encouragement towards women to emulate the holy mothers of the past; but changes to give a severe warning to husbands. It's a lack of respect towards women, he reveals, that hinders prayer:

'Likewise, husbands, live with your wives in an understanding way, showing honour to the woman as the weaker vessel, since they are heirs with you of the grace of life, so that your prayers may not be hindered.'

1 Peter 3:7 ESV

In these words is another, even more subtle, allusion to the incident of the golden calf. Before this event happened, the men of Israel had had the privilege of being priests in their own households. They were entitled to offer prayer directly to God on behalf of themselves and their families.[9]

But after their lapse into idolatry, that honour was stripped from them. It was given to the tribe of Levi—the only ones who heeded the call of Moses when he asked them to side with God.

For over a millennium and a half, ordinary husbands no longer had unhindered access to heaven with their sacrifices—instead they had to make their offerings through the Levites serving in the Tabernacle. When the priesthood was restored through the cross of Jesus, it was one of all believers—women included.

So there's the remarkable nuance in what Peter writes: he equates the respect given to wives with the honour due to God.

According to Jewish teaching, while God punished the men of Israel, He rewarded the women. In perpetuity—that is, as an everlasting memorial for their repeated faithfulness at Mount Sinai—Jewish tradition records that God gifted women with their own special holiday. Once a month, on the day of the New Moon, women are to get the day off. Ladies, I have more than a sneaking suspicion that this is a tribute you've never even heard about before!

In addition, He also gifted the mothers of Israel with long life. Jewish commentary also points out that, when Numbers 26:64–65 speaks of an entire generation who died in the Desert of Sinai, this specifically refers to the men—excepting Caleb and Joshua—and not to the women. Rabbi Eckstein refers us to the original Hebrew, indicating that the verse specifically states: 'not one *man* was left…'

'Why didn't the women die in the desert as the men did?' he asks. 'Is it because God took pity on the women over the men? Not at all. The sages teach that the men had lost their faith on that dreadful night when the spies spoke negatively about the land of Israel—but the women did not. They kept their faith. Even though the spies had reported enemies of large proportions, well-fortified cities, and a land that swallowed its people, the women closed their ears to the men's words. Instead, they opened their hearts to the word of God, who had promised to lead them into a good land. They had passed the test of faith.'[10]

Jewish thought again and again celebrates the faith and faithfulness of the women of Israel. And not just of Israel: to the great frustration of historians, the book of Exodus honours two ordinary Egyptian midwives who feared God by recording their names for posterity while ignoring that of the reigning Pharaoh![11]

Peter's words about braided hair, gold jewellery and clothes can be seen in this light: simply an encouragement towards practical steps that put God first. Just as the holy women of past millennia had done.

So here is one of many hidden treasures of Scripture regarding a mother's blessing: she is to be an example of faithfulness to God. She is to be a model of whole-hearted, unswerving, stand-fast faithfulness which allows God's favour to flow and overflow to her sons and daughters.

Prayer for Myself:

Thank You, heavenly Father, for those women of old who knew Your favour. Please allow us to inherit the blessings and rewards You gave them and teach us to use them for Your glory. Shape our attitudes so that we look critically at the time we spend doing our hair, putting on cosmetics or shopping for clothes or jewellery—and realise that time with You suffers in comparison. Appoint for us practical steps to rectify the imbalance. Cause us to grow, heavenly Father, in faith and faithfulness—give us a double portion of that of those holy women of ages past. Thank You again!

In the name of Your son, Jesus of Nazareth, who is our peace and through the power of His cross to bring us peace. Amen

Prayer for my Children:

El Shaddai, I ask that You show favour to the children You have given me in this family and to their friends. Grant all of them sweetness of days and teach them to honour You so that that they may inherit the blessings You have prepared for them before the beginning of time. Guard their steps so that they may walk, without stumbling or confusion, into the calling that will most satisfy their souls and bring glory to Your name. Remember them all with love, salvation and compassion.

Cause Your presence to dwell in our house. Give to all of us the privilege of knowing You in reverence, in wisdom, in understanding, in truth. Protect us, especially the children, from all who would bully us—physically, emotionally, mentally, spiritually.

Raise up the children You have given me so that they will be light and salt in the world, and that they will love You, be attached to You, set the world afire through the power of Your Word, ready to do the good deeds You appointed for them before the world began.

Heavenly Father, hear my prayer at this time to release Your grace to Your children and all the children of the world.

In the name of Your Son, Jesus of Nazareth, who is our peace and through the power of His cross to bring us peace.

Amen

4
Woman and Mother: Cupbearer

4
Woman and Mother: Cupbearer

WHEN IT COMES TO A READING of Scripture, the full counsel of God should be our standard. All too often we unconsciously allow our cultural biases, historical partiality or generational preferences to sway us. We let our fallen nature dictate how we understand the Word of God. Sometimes we even allow it to rectify Scripture.

Ivan Panin pointed out there are only two passages of any substantial length in the four gospels that are disputed. The earliest manuscript copies we have do not include the last twelve verses of Mark or a major scene in John's gospel.

Common to both these scenes is God's grace to less-than-virtuous women. In the first, Mary Magdalene—notorious as the person who had seven demons cast out of her by Jesus—is honoured by being recorded as the first witness of the resurrection. In the second, a woman caught in the act of adultery is presented to Jesus. Instead of condemning her, He writes in the sand, in some mysterious way shaming her accusers. Once they have left, He offers her forgiveness and a second chance.

Panin has noted that, at least in the case of Mark's gospel, while our earliest *copies* lack the last twelve verses, *even* earlier *writings* refer to them. He suggested that some copyist, like Uzzah who reached out his hand to steady the Ark of the Covenant, felt the need to 'right' the testimony of the apostles when it came to the place of women.[12]

Such remedies continue on, through the centuries, down to our own day. We have seen this in the last section on 'submission'.

Jerram Barrs has commented in *Through His Eyes: God's Perspective on Women* in the Bible on the curse of sin perverting headship into domination. While he commends Nabal's wife, Abigail, for being wise, discerning and generous, he reveals that some Christian pastors have criticised her for *not* submitting to her husband. The fact she saves his life is less important than the fact she went behind his back.

This viewpoint sees 'submission' as unquestioning obedience. Ironically, once we understand the true nature of submission, Abigail is the epitome of it.

Her story is told in 1 Samuel 25. When we first meet her, she's in a quandary. Her home was about to be destroyed and her husband killed. For many months, Nabal's property, livestock and workers had been protected from marauders—both two-legged and four-legged—by a band of volunteers. David and his men were camped nearby and, as part of a good neighbour policy, they kept a lookout for thieves and predators. Of course, this increased security—especially because it was unpaid—meant that Nabal was able to increase his business profits substantially. He was already wealthy but all the surveillance by David's men made him more so.

The day came when David and his men ran short of supplies and they decided to ask Nabal for help. After all, Nabal had grown richer off the back of their efforts. David wasn't asking for wages; just sufficient food to tide his men over. But his messengers were rebuffed. Nabal unwisely added a few offensive comments about David to cap off his refusal.

When David heard what Nabal had said, he was insulted. 'To your swords!' he said to his followers.

When Abigail heard what Nabal had said, she just knew David would be insulted. She knew she had to move fast to avoid a massacre.

Risking her life, she set off to save her husband and his workers. When she intercepted David and his men, offering them a whole range of fine provisions, David calmed down and recognised how deeply he was indebted to her. In his rage, he would have killed Nabal.

Eventually, when he heard what a close-run thing the whole episode had been, Nabal had a heart attack and died a few days later.

Regardless of Nabal's eventual fate in this story, Abigail protects both men. She acts to directly shield Nabal from the consequences of his action. In doing so, she also indirectly shields David from the consequences of his reaction. David realises she's stopped him from committing murder and is deeply thankful.

Abigail is the perfect example of a paraclete who uses initiative, takes risks to defend those for whom she's responsible, and shields her husband from the battle he's provoked. Ironically those who accuse her of not being submissive to her husband have missed the reality of true submission as an act of protection. In acting as her husband's 'armour-bearer', she becomes the 'keeper of the head' and the 'one who provides covering' as well as the 'one who lifts up'.

Just as a cupbearer tests the king's drink to protect his life, Abigail stands in harm's way to prevent both Nabal and David from regretting the consequences of their sinful actions and reactions.

In providing bread, meat and fruit for David's men, she goes in with weapons to protect the lives of her husband and her household. This battleground is not metaphorical; it is very real. In fact the Hebrew word for *bread*, 'lehem', is the same as the word for *war*. (Yes, Bethlehem, *house of bread*, could just as validly be translated *house of war*.)

Here is the true role wives are called to: to be *tenderly devoted*, as Brian Simmons translated 'submit', as a battle partner and also to have the wisdom to know when warfare is better conducted with a bread roll than a sword.

Much later, after David has become king, another woman saves him from the full consequences of a terrible mistake. After three years of famine, David realised that God was not answering prayer on behalf of the drought-stricken land. So he asked heaven: 'Why?'

The answer God gave him is that his predecessor, Saul, all but wiped out the people of Gibeon, breaking the covenant that Joshua had cut with them centuries previously. David went to the Gibeonite survivors and asked what they wanted.

Not surprisingly, they wanted revenge.

Very surprisingly, David allowed them to have it.

In violation of his own covenant with Saul and Jonathan—which specified he had to take care of their families as long as he lived—he betrayed his vows. He handed over members of Saul's family and allowed the Gibeonites to put them to death. Only the actions of Saul's concubine, Rizpah, awakened David's conscience.[13] It seems he was brought to sincere repentance of his action. Otherwise, the cycle of disaster for covenant-breaking would have kept rolling forward.

A cup-bearer doesn't just stand in harm's way. A true cup-bearer awakens conscience.

As women and mothers, that's what we're called to do.

Prayer for Myself:

Heavenly Father, grant me wisdom, discernment and generosity whenever I am called to resolve conflict and be a 'keeper of the head', an armour-bearer, a paraclete, a battle companion who provides cover and protection, a covenant defender, a cup-bearer. In whatever situation I find myself, empower me with Your grace to fulfil the command of Jesus to be 'subtle as serpents and gentle as doves'.

Father, I ask that Your gracious Son, Jesus of Nazareth, be the keeper of my head, my armour-bearer, my paraclete, my battle companion, my cover and protection, my covenant defender and also my cup-bearer. I also ask that Your Holy Spirit be the keeper of my head, my armour-bearer, my paraclete, my battle companion, my cover and protection, my covenant defender and also my cup-bearer.

I am willing, Father, to be a channel of peace and forgiveness to those who have despised women and their role in Your kingdom. Allow the forgiveness Your Son showed to so many women during His time here on earth to flow through me to others. Make me an instrument of raising up both men and women so they can fulfil the Kingdom purposes You have called them to.

And, as You are my covenant defender, I ask Your protection over my loved ones. Send angels, I pray, to stand defensive watch over every member of my family. May they also guard those gifts and possessions You have entrusted to me for the task of lifting up others to glorify Your name.

Lord, help me to be a woman who lifts others up and rouses the conscience of those around me to keep covenant with You. Help me especially to lift up Your name and to honour You before my family, my friends, my community and the world.

In the name of Jesus of Nazareth, my armour-bearer, my armour-giver, my watchman and my cupbearer.

Amen

Prayer for my Children:

Abba Father, I present Your child to You and ask that You would help Your beloved one to be strengthened daily and to learn to lean into You and Your grace.

Bless Your child with the ability to yield wholeheartedly to Your plan and purpose. Abba Father, watch over this child bringing love, joy, peace, patience, kindness, goodness, gentleness, faithfulness and self-control to their spirit as they mature through the development stages.

Forbid that Your child should be tossed back and forth with the waves of life and circumstances but, however great the turbulence, grant them a strong anchor in You. Grant to them knowledge of their true identity and also the wisdom to be able to step forward to the destiny You have for them.

Lord, will You help to restore and regulate emotions and healthy relationship bonds for Your child. I ask that You bring quiet and rest to their spirit and soul at those times when they become overwhelmed or distressed, or stuck in anger and rage.

Abba Father, please remove the trauma of extreme emotions from Your child and lift off any shame which comes from their emotional responses. Father, I ask You to show Your child how to experience joy and to allow them to find friends who can love them in their community.

I pray asking that, today, a gift of faith be imparted to this child as well as courage to face any unforgiving feelings and thoughts hidden inside through shame, trauma or fear.

I pray Abba Father will release strength to this child to believe in Him for Hebrews 11:5 says, '*And without faith it is impossible to please God, because anyone who comes to Him must believe that He exists and that He rewards those who earnestly seek Him.'*

I pray, Abba Father, that You will pour Your grace down today so that Your child can please You, simply by believing in You.

In the name of Jesus of Nazareth, who makes it possible for us to receive the grace to believe.

Amen

5
Woman and Mother: Game-changer

5
Woman and Mother: Game-changer

ABIGAIL AND RIZPAH ARE FAR from the first women to change events for good.

At the beginning of Exodus, God isn't mentioned at all. At the beginning of Genesis, the book just before it, His presence is inescapable. However the second book of the Bible starts out in an apparent spiritual void.

Andrew Reid says: '…in the absence of God, five women make their presence known… If there are heroes in the text, it is these, for they act to preserve God's future for his people through protecting male children in general and Moses in particular.'[14]

Two ordinary women—midwives—are so honoured in Jewish history that they are named while Pharaoh's daughter is not. In fact, to the great frustration of generations of historians, even the name of the reigning Pharaoh is omitted. By failing to preserve it, the worst nightmare of an Egyptian ruler has come to pass: that of having their name obliterated, their very existence erased, by their successors.

To begin with, the midwives Shiphrah and Puah are given such prominence that they appear more important than the sister and mother of Moses—Miriam and Jochebed. Those two pivotal women remain unnamed for several chapters.

The motif of women as agents of rescue and salvation is an ongoing one. When Moses is returning to Egypt, another woman saves him from destruction. Her action in fact foreshadows God's covenant defence during the first Passover as she uses blood to fend off the divinely appointed Angel of Death.

In one of the most mysterious episodes in Scripture, God sends an attack against His own chosen messenger, after having just commissioned him to lead the Israelites out of Egypt. Moses is on his way to Egypt with his wife Zipporah and his son Gershom. They are going at God's command to confront Pharaoh and on the way, Moses stops and enters an inn.

There an angel tries to kill him. Only Zipporah's swift action in circumcising one of the males (it's unclear whether it was Gershom or Moses she circumcised) saved their lives.

This seemingly bizarre episode is comprehensible once we recognise that, when Moses stepped over the threshold stone and accepted hospitality at the inn, he came into covenant with the host.

Clearly that covenant had to be a betrayal of God.[15] A treachery so enormous that His protection was no longer in force. When Zipporah intervened by using a covenant token to reaffirm loyalty to God, the assault was over—apparently as abruptly as it began.

Here is yet another example like several we've seen previously: it highlights the faithfulness of the women in contrast to the faithlessness of the men. It is a recurring theme of Exodus—a theme entirely obscured in English translations.

This unwavering loyalty of the women foreshadows that of those who stood at the foot of the cross and who, on the third day after that sky-shattering, earth-shaking event, made their way to the tomb with spices to anoint the body of Jesus. Thus they were the first to embrace the reality of the Resurrection.

Similarly, back in Exodus, we see women are the first to embrace the covenant at Mount Sinai. We have already also noted they did not make any offerings for the golden calf but were the first to make gold offerings for the Tabernacle.

They also handed over the brass mirrors they'd been given by the Egyptian women to be reforged into the vast laver, the washing basin, for the Tabernacle entrance. *'When Moses finished setting up the tabernacle, he anointed and consecrated it and all its furnishings. He also anointed and consecrated the altar and all its utensils.'* (Numbers 7:1 NIV)

Yechiel Eckstein comments on this particular verse: 'the word chosen by Scripture for *finished*, "kalot", can also mean *bride*. One reason for the allusion to a bride at this juncture in time is because the children of Israel were the bride and God the groom; the completed Tabernacle would be their shared home. However, there is another significance to this word with a double meaning. While "kalot" describes an *ending*, it also points to a *beginning*. A bride is a symbol of a new beginning as a woman begins a new life with her marriage. The word "kalot", with its opposite connotations, teaches us that every end is also a beginning.'[16]

It seems strange but here in the verse about Moses finishing the setting up of the Tabernacle, we already have a foretaste of what it would mean for Jesus to finish His work of redemption and become the firstfruits of those to be resurrected.

Here also in this verse we see the consequences of the mothers of Israel remaining steadfast, while the men continually wavered. The completion of the Tabernacle paved the way for a new beginning. The women's faithfulness made a difference time after time. As mentioned previously, God treated them differently: for example, in Exodus 19:3–6 he instructed Moses to speak to women with gentle encouragement and to men with stern admonition.

As a result of the golden calf incident, ordinary men lost the right to be priests in their own household. Levites were excepted, because they sided with Moses when he called for the people to come back to God. This right was eventually restored through the work of Jesus. But it was no longer exclusive. All believers were invited to share in the priestly work of Jesus.

'There is no longer Jew or Gentile, slave or free, male and female. For you are all one in Christ Jesus.' (Galatians 3:28 NLT)

Now naturally, not all Jewish men were as inclusive as Jesus. Many were as misogynistic as the Greeks. Today, largely in keeping with our Greek rationalist heritage, we still relegate women to second place. Some denominations restrict the priesthood to men and, even amongst those that don't, the average conference line-up reveals an interesting preservation of privilege.

The problem with having a skewed view of the value of the feminine—or the masculine—is simple. We are perpetuating the separation of man and woman that occurred at the Fall. Instead of embracing the covenantal oneness of the Bride with her Redeemer.

When women are dishonoured, prayers are hindered and remain unanswered. '...*she is your equal partner in God's gift of new life. Treat her as you should, so your prayers will not be hindered.*' (1 Peter 3:7 NLT)

On the other hand, when men are dishonoured, their authority is weakened and their covering protection is muted.

Mutual honour reflects the design God has for marriage: uplifting and upbuilding each other in love so that the world itself begins to mend.

Prayer for Myself:

Lord, thank You for the example of the women who were game-changers and risked their lives for others. Grant me a soul as brave and fearless as theirs. When laws are proposed that put the vulnerable and defenceless at risk, particularly children and the unborn, strengthen my resolve to reverence You and fight on their behalf, more than I might fear any human reaction.

Lord, thank You for the example of the mothers who came up with ideas and plans to save their children from dangerous situations. Grant to me ideas that safeguard others and provide me with the materials to put those ideas into action.

Lord, thank You for the example of the women who were faithful to You; who stood firm despite those falling away and showed the community what true commitment meant. Grant to me a steadfast heart that honours You in all I do.

Lord, where I have dishonoured others, I name them now before You.

I repent of the thoughts of my heart and the words of my mouth, Lord. Through the power of Your Cross, I ask You to blot out those words of dishonour wherever they may have lodged or been recorded—in the hearts and minds of those I dishonoured, in the scrolls of Heaven, the records of hell, in any place on the earth or in the fabric of the universe where such dishonour may be registered. Lord, let my words and thoughts of dishonour be as the name of Pharaoh—erased forever.

Lord, cleanse me of anything that hinders my prayer to You. Wash me and remove anything that weakens the authority of those over me—and thus weakens my own authority.

Cover me, as Your bride, with Your banner of love. Help me to do all I can to work with You in mending the world.

In the name of Jesus and through the power of His cross and by the righteousness given through His precious blood.

Amen

Prayer to speak over my children:

Beloved daughter, beloved son, child of God, it's my sincere honour to bless you and pray over you as a mother.

Pour nurture and comfort, Holy Spirit; I ask that You would come now and give this, Your child, Your gift of peace and comfort. You alone are the comforter and counsellor and, Lord, I ask You to remove any trauma of neglect—for not being blessed and called forth into the identity and destiny that You designed for this child from the beginning of time.

Pour refreshment and security into this child, Holy Spirit. I ask that You would come now and give Your gift of peace and strength. Lord, I ask that Jesus and the Holy Spirit, our advocates, would bring Your child into Your heavenly courts. Heavenly advocates, please stand by Your child, as You, Lord God, judge and address all wounds that the enemy has inflicted.

Lord, please call into order any parts of heart, soul, body or mind that have been affected by forces of chaos or destruction and close any open access of the Enemy to Your child.

Abba Father, I ask that You send Your Holy Spirit to brood over this precious child, to displace darkness and trauma and bring your light and life today. Again, I ask for the Kiss of Heaven which is the armour of God to be over this child and surround this precious life with your protection and peace.

In the name of Jesus, our mediator and advocate, who made it possible to enter Your courts.

Amen

6
Woman and Mother: Gatekeeper

6
Woman and Mother: Gatekeeper

SOME PEOPLE STRUGGLE WITH THE Bible as historical—they don't believe it can be verified by archaeology or ancient documents. Other people struggle with its contents—with a God who seems bloodthirsty; with its prescriptive directions for worship and right living; with its domineering view of women.

For many years, I struggled with a different problem—the way it's written. I'm an avid reader and I love fairytales, adventures and speculative fiction with interwoven romantic elements that finally tie together in a poignant, satisfying ending. My favourite kind of story is that of the hidden prince who overcomes incredible obstacles to win his kingdom and wed the heroine. The emotional rush at the end of such books is what I'm looking for to feed something deep within.

On several occasions I said to God that I felt I should feel the same way about the Bible. Isn't it the happiest of happily-ever-afters imaginable? So why didn't I experience the same fulfilling touch when it came to Scripture? Was it something wrong in me?

I'm reasonably sure this is not a question a man would ever ask God. I can't see a male fronting Him with the thought the Bible doesn't pack as much emotional punch as a soppy romance novel. I can't see a man feeling a sense of disquiet over the matter. In general men tend to seek intellectual satisfaction, remaining content with that.

However I'm glad I asked God the question. Over a period of years, He dropped a series of clues that led me into a different way of reading. I discovered the Bible is meant to be spiritually, emotionally and intellectually satisfying.

And the romance of the hidden king coming into His kingdom and winning His bride was there all along. To find it, it's necessary to follow the storyline of the bride in the garden.

The first bride found in a garden is Eve, *the mother of all living*.

Born from the side of Adam, she was flesh of his flesh, bone of his bone.

'*Women were created from the rib of man to be beside him, not from his head to top him, nor from his feet to be trampled by him, but from under his arm to be protected by him, near to his heart to be loved by him.*'

Matthew Henry, *An Exposition of the Old and New Testament*

Adam and Eve were so completely caught up in harmonious oneness with each other and with God that it doesn't seem to have occurred to either of them she was a separate being. And she wasn't at the start. They were 'one flesh'.

She didn't even receive the name Eve until after both of them were expelled from Eden. Before that, she was 'the other Adam'.

Marriage under the headship of Christ is meant to restore this deep oneness in a kiss of peace, mercy, justice and truth.

We all know the story of Eve and the serpent. What many people forget is that Scripture records her as duped and deceived.[17] Adam on the other hand knew precisely what he was doing. Throughout

Scripture, he is the one to bear the responsibility for the first sin.

How does Eve's gullibility affect the way we understand the serpent's presentation to her? What did she understand by the serpent's suggestion that God's test wasn't what they thought it was? How did she interpret the line: 'You will be like gods'? After all, she and Adam were already *one with God*.

Here is the subtlety of the serpent's invitation. To 'be like' implies separation; whereas God's intention was always that we be 'one with' Him.

Are we called to be like God? Not if 'likeness' is different from 'oneness'.

In Colossians 1:15, when Paul talks about Christ being in the likeness and image of God, he immediately clarifies his meaning by referring to the Body. This is therefore not a mirror likeness which implies separation between persons. Rather it is a likeness that refers to the oneness between God, ourselves and Christ. This likeness also refers to the oneness between ourselves as individuals and the Body of Christ, His church.

This oneness is the very essence of covenant. It is the purpose of covenant. It is what differentiates covenant from contract.

There are four types of covenant: blood, salt, name and threshold. Many people are familiar with the existence of the first two, even when they are unfamiliar with the implications of the oneness that characterises them.[18] Most people however have never even heard of the last two. Despite so many women actually having participated in a name covenant. Every woman who has changed her name on marriage has undertaken one. The ancient purpose of such a commitment is to give full family privileges to one another, including inheritance rights. In addition, they agree to be mutual covenant defenders.

Jesus Himself instituted a name covenant for His followers on the night before He died. *'Until now you have not asked for anything in My name. Ask and you will receive, and your joy will be complete.'* (John 16:24 NIV) He explains that we are not to ask Him but to ask the Father in His name.

This was part of the fourfold covenant of blood, salt, threshold and name that took place over a period of half a day, culminating in a betrothal between Himself and His new-born bride.

Hints about this marriage have existed all the way through John's gospel, from the wedding feast of Cana onwards. This gospel has a very unusual literary design. It has a mirror structure: at the beginning John testifies to Jesus, the lamb of God. At the end, another John testifies to Jesus, who spoke of lambs and sheep. At the start, five disciples, including Simon Peter and Nathanael, follow Jesus to Galilee. At the end, five groups of disciples, including Simon Peter and Nathanael, follow Jesus to Galilee, At the start, Nathanael expresses doubts while, at the end, Thomas expresses doubts. At the start, there is an incident at a wedding involving a woman named Mary. At the end, there is an incident involving bridal language[19] involving a different woman named Mary. Common to both of these incidents is that Jesus stops and alters His plans. He says in John 4:4 that it's not yet the right time for Him to go public but He stops, listens to the distress of His mother and changes His plans. In John 20:17, He reveals He is on His way to His Father—but He has stopped on the way and changed His plan to comfort Mary Magdalene in her distress.

The mirroring goes on and on. Each of these reflective incidents is clearly meant to inform, and be informed by, its matching partner. Perhaps the most significant pairing involves Nicodemus.

His first appearance is in the third chapter of John where we are told he met secretly with Jesus. Instead of getting his questions answered, he was offered some cryptic statements about being reborn. The whole idea of 'new birth' messed with his mind. Images of having to crawl back into his mother's womb surfaced.

Jesus clarified for him: '*I tell you the truth, no one can enter the Kingdom of God unless he is born of water and the Spirit.*' (John 3:5 NIV)

No doubt Nicodemus remained baffled about this very helpful new statement: what would the breaking of the waters of a spiritual childbirth look like?

The final appearance of Nicodemus occurs at the end of John's gospel right after this statement: '...*one of the soldiers pierced His side with a spear, and immediately blood and water came out.*' (John 19:34 NIV)

Blood and water. The same elements as at a birth. Perhaps Nicodemus recognised what was happening—that, as he watched Jesus' side being pierced, he was actually witnessing a birth. Particularly since the word for *blood* used in this verse is 'haima'—also meaning *spirit*.

Admittedly it's not the same word Jesus used back in John 3:5 for *spirit*. That was 'pneuma'. However, the testimony of the ring-like structural design tells us that these two stories are linked. Nicodemus was probably more baffled than ever as he witnessed a breaking forth of water and blood/spirit, the very things Jesus had explained accompanied the new birth.

For a start, Jesus had just said, 'It is finished,' and died. And secondly, birth doesn't normally occur through a man's pierced side.

It's not impossible, but it's certainly not usual. Only one similar instance had ever occurred previously in all of recorded history: when Eve was born. As woman was taken from the side of the first Adam, so the Bride was taken from the second Adam—Jesus Christ.

Nicodemus, as an observant Jew, would have got the significance of the new birth in that moment. 'It is finished,' Jesus said. In Aramaic, this is 'kalah'. Brian Simmons in the Passion Translation points out this sounds just like 'kallah', *bride*.[20] Even in His last words, Jesus was thinking of us—His bride—as we were about to be 'born again' of water and the spirit.

Does this still mess with your head as Jesus' words once messed with Nicodemus'?

The way through into new birth, to becoming a Christian, to following Jesus of Nazareth, to entering a covenantal relationship with Him as His bride is to enter His wounded side by faith. In practice, there's been a tendency to reverse this process in the last century or so: the process of being 'born again' has been seen as inviting Jesus into our hearts instead of accepting His invitation to be hidden in His.

Kenneth Leech points out there's a power structure in all this. 'It sought to bring Jesus into our lives instead of bringing us into His. The gospel as preached in the west no longer helped to turn the world upside down but rather served to reinforce its false values and structures.'[21]

Are you ready to embrace the romance and recognise Jesus as the Bridegroom? Are you willing to ask Him if He would invite you into the new birth—His life—through His pierced and wounded side?

Prayer for myself:

Lord Jesus—I simply want to be taken into You. Hidden in You. Born anew in You, through Your wounded side.

I want to dance with You. Dance the *hora*. I want to be uplifted with You as Your bride. I want to be on a throne swaying above the rejoicing angels—and I want You to throw out to me that cloth You laid neatly to one side in the tomb. The cloth that says, 'My work is finished,' and whispers that You have chosen me as Your bride.

I throw down my crown before You and acknowledge, 'Holy, holy, holy.' That's what You are and what You're making me.

Thank You!

Prayer over my children:

El Shaddai, thanks be to You for giving the peace and power that this child needs. Thank you for Your blessing and refreshing that rests as a gift of grace over this child today.

I love my children so much but I do not want to love them more than I love you—so I present their lives and destinies to you.

I ask that You release them into their destiny in You. I ask that You help them choose that destiny, not turn away from it or from You. I ask that, until the time of the revealing of their destiny, that they be hidden in You—in Your wounded side.

I thank you for the privilege of raising these precious children—lives that You ordained and blessed. I ask that You untangle them from me in any way that I have sought my needs instead of theirs. I ask You to unbind them from me and bind them to Yourself as the source of their life.

Bless them to be unique and independent. May they always know how much I love and care for them—and, as long as I live, I will declare the goodness of the Lord in the land of the living. Bless my children today to declare Your goodness and mercy in their lifetime for Your glory.

Amen

7
Woman and Mother: Above Pearls

7
Woman and Mother: Above Pearls

The gospels do not record her name. A very early tradition suggests she was a Gentile called Veronica and that she came from Caesarea Philippi.[22] After Jesus healed her of more than a decade of suffering, she was so grateful she commissioned a statue of Him that, for centuries, stood beside the doorway of her house. It was renowned as the only likeness of the Messiah made during His lifetime.[23]

This is the woman with the 'issue of blood'. For twelve years she spent all her money on doctors, trying to find a cure for her chronic haemorrhaging. Nothing worked. In desperation, she travelled to Capernaum, seeking a Man named Jesus. His reputation as a miracle-worker, a teacher and a healer had made Him a celebrity.

Now if Veronica was indeed a Gentile, she was nonetheless aware of Jewish religious law. She obviously knew she was 'unclean' and could not afford to brave a crowd and bare her problem publicly. However, if she was also from out of town—from Caesarea Philippi in the far north—she had an advantage. No one would know her problem, so she could make her way secretly through the crowd and—just as secretly—touch the hem of Jesus' garment.

Her plan was carefully crafted. If she could get close enough to brush her hand against one of the tassels on his prayer shawl—one of the *tzitzit*, the symbol of his prayer-connection to the Jewish God, the source of His power—no one would ever know. In the jostling press of people surrounding Him, who would ever notice such a light, casual touch? She would not reach out to Jesus Himself, but only to the 'wings' of His garment. If Jesus were truly the Messiah, then He was the One with healing in His wings. It was a risk well worth taking.

She had nothing to lose. If she didn't receive healing, she would be no worse off. With everything to gain and nothing to lose, she set out. For the plan to work, it would be necessary to join a moving crowd and negotiate her way through it towards Jesus. In a static crowd, she'd be too obvious. Events favoured her that day. Jesus was on His way to the house of the leader of the synagogue. A little girl was on the point of death.

But Veronica was stuck in 'death'—and had been for the entire length of time the little girl had been alive.

The flow of life runs through well-known seasons. When a grain of wheat falls to the ground, it 'dies' in order to bring to birth a green shoot which grows to maturity, only to 'die' as the cycle begins again with a multiplication of seeds. Rebirth, growth, death, new life, multiplication, on and on through the cycle. At any point, there is the potentiality of loss—into a permanent death, one where rebirth is impossible.

The spiritual life cycle for people is very similar:

But what happens when we get stuck in a part of the cycle? This is basically what had happened to Veronica. Her story occurs in the three synoptic gospels—Matthew, Mark and Luke—where it is clear from the description of her disease that she was 'unclean'. This is not uncleanness as we would understand it—dirty or defiled—but rather uncleanness as being ritually or ceremonially untouchable. In many respects, 'unclean' here has the same sense as 'taboo' originally did—contact is forbidden because, to do so, is to violate the sacred.

The Hebrew word for *uncleanness* here is 'tumah'—a word also connected with birth. *Uncleanness* has the sense of *emptiness*. The womb was 'tumah' when a child was born because it had been emptied of life. After the birth of a son, a Jewish mother was set apart for a week; for a girl, it was a fortnight. The period of 'tumah' was greater for a daughter because the birth of a girl is seen as resulting in a greater emptiness.

That may seem strange but there's a certain logic to it. A baby girl effectively brings all her potential grandchildren into the world at her birth. Infant daughters are born with all their eggs, but infant boys are not born with all their sperm.

A little boy does not have the potential for life—in the form of children from his own body—within him at birth, whereas a little girl does. She also has the potential for more and more death. Hence why the time of 'tumah' for a daughter was twice as long as for a son.

The true sense of 'tumah' is that of a void of potential, an emptying, a giving out, a sacrifice—the experience of a loss that is not yet fully lost. It's unfinished, unreconciled. To be 'unclean' is to suffer a loss without closure, without resolution. It's to be in a season void of life.

The Jewish laws pertaining to menstruation were a celebration of the marvellous cycle of life happening within a woman. They are meant as a constant reminder of the miracle of daily existence—and to realise the function of our physical bodies is wondrous, not disgusting or even routine. The Jewish laws are there to enable us to realise the awe-inspiring potential of life as it regenerates itself within our very own bodies.

But sometimes things go wrong. We don't pass through the natural seasons in their ordained order and timing. It's no coincidence that 'dumah', *silence*, rhymes with 'tumah'. The silence of death, mourning, grief and God Himself after the breaking of covenant are themes threaded through the Scriptural record.[24]

When Veronica touches the wings of Jesus' prayer shawl, she comes instantly 'unstuck' from the death stage where she'd been pinioned for twelve years. Her losses are instantly resolved and she is able to move into the next season of life. No longer is she like a 'dead man walking' but she's alive to potential again. It's as if her defaults are reset and she comes back to zero once more, instead of constantly being drained into the negative. It's as if she's been like a lifeless seed, buried in the ground for twelve years, and her regeneration has begin.

Jesus heals her—not simply of a constant haemorrhage, but of a loss that she could find no one to help her resolve. When loss comes to us, especially when silence surrounds that loss and we can find no answers for it, then we can end up with all sorts of conditions—physical, emotional and spiritual—that drain life from us. We bleed constantly. It's not that we're not plugged into Jesus but that we're constantly being sucked dry of the resurrection life and its fullness that He promised.

Whether it's people, organisation, land—whatever our loss, it takes the fruit of the Spirit from us, squeezes out the juice and leaves us with the dessicated rind.

This is the very opposite of the woman of valour in Proverbs 31 and who she is meant to be. She meant to move gracefully within the life flow, not be stuck somewhere—unable to progress. Although most English translations compare her worth above that of rubies, the Hebrew text compares her to a pearl.[25]

The difference between the pearl and the ruby reveals the true nature of a woman of uniquely noble character. A ruby is a naturally occurring gemstone, created by reactive chemical processes. A pearl, however, is created through organic means and begins with an irritation. A speck of sand, an attacking parasite, even a damaged part of the oyster itself is coated with a creamy seal, building layer upon layer, until a beautiful, smooth and rare treasure is formed.

A woman who has overcome the annoyances, torments and trauma to develop a serene loveliness of personality is a woman of pearl-like grandeur. Like Mary, the mother of Jesus, to whom it was prophesied that a sword would pierce her soul, many women have felt the stabs and spearthrusts of sudden, tragic loss. Or worse, the long slow agony of watching a loved one die or a relationship head into irreversible damage.

These are the 'tumah' losses.

Yet, as the result of such adversity, the woman who is more precious than pearls has soft edges, not hard faceted ones—she's been crafted into a different sort of gemstone altogether.

She's become a jewel through adding, layer on layer, as Peter advised in his second epistle, goodness to her faith; and to that goodness, knowledge; and to her knowledge, self-control; and to her self-control perseverance; and to her perseverance godliness; and to her godliness kindness and to her kindness, love.

That's the rare and transcendent beauty God sees when He looks down on our 'tumah' and 'dumah'—our death-loss and our silence—as He waits for us to turn and seek His healing.

He sees a pearl. And, despite our feelings of alienation and distance from Him, that pearl is an ornament that He's always worn close to His heart.

Prayer for myself:

Oh, Lord, I'm stuck in that place of silence. Stuck in the place of loss. The loss that goes on, without resolution, without explanation, almost without hope of change.

I'm so afraid that I can't even risk touching the hem of Your garment in case I don't get healed, in case the loss continues without closure, in case the emptiness—the deep aching hollow void—remains unfilled.

Dear Jesus, please take my hand and bring it up to touch the fringe of Your prayer shawl. My prayers have been worthless for so long—but Yours are not. I ask that You are my only mediator before the Father and I ask You to dismiss all others I may have put in Your place over the years.

Please close my wound. Staunch the flow of life. And bring me to the next season on my journey with You.

In the name of Jesus, the Sun of Righteousness who rises with healing in His wings.

Amen

Prayer for my child:

Lord, I ask You bless Your child today with contentment, to be hidden in You—at peace during the storms of life. El Shaddai, bless the children You have given me to reach out to You and snuggle into Your arms in times of pain and disappointment.

May they draw strength from You alone. Reveal to them false refuges, expose those places they run to instead of to You, the author and finisher of faith, the Alpha and Omega of all creation.

Lord, You are a jealous God. You want all of us—our whole heart, soul and mind. In Matthew 22:37 (NIV), Jesus said the greatest commandment is: 'Love the Lord your God with all your heart and with all your soul and with all your mind.'

El Shaddai, gift and grace Your child with Your strength to live in a way that honours You, to make the decisions to follow You, to choose You each and every day—and not be caught in the trappings of this world. Instead of choosing consuming and consumption—the God of this world—may Your child choose what You desire and have the courage to lift up the name of the great 'I am'.

Lord, You put before us the same choices that You put before the people of Israel in the time of Joshua:

This day I call the heavens and the earth as witnesses against you that I have set before you life and death, blessings and curses. Now choose life, so that you and your children may live.

Deuteronomy 30:19 (NIV)

El Shaddai, I ask You to bless Your children today in order that they may choose life, choose You as their Lord and Saviour and draw wisdom and understanding from You, allow You to be their teacher.

Child, if your parents have forsaken you, or abandoned you or left you without all that you need, then turn to Jesus and to El Shaddai, the mighty, and ask Him to comfort you just as you need and long for from your parents.

Lord, when substances, addictions, people, hobbies, work and distractions have diverted Your children away from your loving embrace, will You draw them back and lift off from them the trauma? Will You also fill the longings and unmet needs that only You can satisfy?

May Your children's hearts be purified to carry the presence and peace of the One who formed them and who fashioned them into His likeness more and more each day—and may your covenant of peace rule their hearts forever.

For Your glory alone. In Jesus' name.

Amen

Endnotes

Endnotes

1. Unicef advises: 'We know that babies who have spent an hour in skin contact are significantly less stressed after the birth experience—this means their breathing and heart rate are more stable, they cry less, and when they start to feed, they digest their food better. A mother's chest area is significantly warmer than other parts of her body—ready to welcome her new baby and prevent them from cooling down—which is a significant risk. Your baby has been lovely and warm in your uterus—at around 37 degrees, whereas the labour room will be significantly cooler, and he is wet—it's like getting out of the swimming baths, you need to get dry and warm quickly.'

    Jamie's parents, the Oggs, have set up an online community called *Jamie's Gift* to regularly raise funds for the *Miracle Babies Foundation*—an organisation that supports premature and sick newborns.

    http://www.dailymail.co.uk/news/article-2992862/The-miracle-baby-born-three-months-early-written-doctors-brought-life-mother-s-touch-five-years-old-s-never-sick.html (accessed 15/10/15)

2. God made us so that, when we touch one another with kindness and affection, our bodies produce chemicals that create emotional calm and assist with physical bonding. These chemicals are oxytocin and dopamine. When we hug,

oxytocin is released by our pituitary glands. This lowers both heart rate and our level of cortisol, the hormone responsible for stress and high blood pressure. Dopamine is a hormone that gives us a sense of pleasure.

3   It has many other overtones too, including *lift off*, *support*, *forgive*, *carry*, *bear arms*, *sustain*, *deliver up*, *endure*. But significantly, like 'hupotasso', it's also means *submit*.

4   The Aramaic 'nasiyn', *wives*, is said to derive from "enash', *man*, *mankind*, which is derived from "enowsh', *mortal*, *man*, *men*, *mankind*, which is in turn derived from "anash', *weak*, *sick*, *incurable*. It seems to me, however, that it is far more likely 'nasiyn', *wives*, comes from 'nasu', *married*, and is actually derived from 'nasa", *to lift up*.

5   I had always imagined the end of the battle being towards sundown; however some Jewish commentaries describe it as being just prior to daybreak. What Joshua asks for, in the view of some rabbis, is the sun not to rise!

6   Yechiel Eckstein, 'By the Light of the Moon', *Holy Land Moments Daily Devotional*, 19 February 2014. Eckstein goes on to explain that the women were rewarded for this attitude with a monthly holiday. Every new moon there is a mini-holiday exclusively for the women.

7   And when it comes to blessing, this connection between Jacob and his grandmother might account for one of the most mysterious titles in Scripture: the House of Jacob.

Then Moses went up to God, and the Lord called to him from the mountain and said, 'This is what you are to say to the house of Jacob and … tell the people of Israel: "You yourselves have seen what I did to Egypt … Now if you obey Me fully and keep My covenant, then … you will be My treasured possession …"' (Exodus 19:3–6 NIV)

According to some rabbis (see, for example, David Patterson in *Hebrew Language and Jewish Thought*) the House of Jacob in this passage is not synonymous with the people of Israel. Although it's poetic parallelism, this does not necessarily mean that the phrases refer to the same set of people. These rabbis identify the House of Jacob as specifically referring to 'the women of the tribes of Israel' and suggest the text indicates that, at Mount Sinai, the women stepped forward first to accept the covenant of the Law. The Israelite men, still smarting over the golden calf, were slow to follow that lead.

8   English translations just use 'say' without any differentiation. However, the article Gender in medieval and modern Jewish translation of Exodus 19:3—House of Jacob and Children/Sons of Israel (bit.ly/1mVUehY) explores the widespread Jewish notion that 'House of Jacob' refers to the Israelite women and notes the very different verbs used; one is gentle exhortation, the other is stern and echoing with punishment.

9   This priesthood came from that of Adam and Eve. Their priesthood over creation was part of their God-given purpose and identity. That restored priesthood is today given to all believers as part of our calling. We are to *represent God to our world* through ministering the Gospel and *represent it back to Him* through prayer.

10 Yechiel Eckstein, 'Passing the Tests of Faith', *Holy Land Moments Daily Devotional*, 7 July 2015

11 Puah and Shiphrah: see chapter 5.

12 Ivan Panin's magisterial mathematical analysis of these verses includes a comparison with the opening verses of the same gospel, showing both have the same 'numerical signature'.

13 And perhaps brought him to repentance.

14 Andrew Reid, 'Exodus: Saved for Service', *Reading the Bible Today* series, Aquila Press Sydney 2013. Reid goes on to say: …on a significant number of occasions [throughout Scripture], the background to their godly action is the failure of male leadership or the absence of God-fearing men.'

15 The unusual Hebrew word for *inn*, *lodging place* or *khan* used in this instance was perhaps chosen because it could be read with the word for *treachery* within it. 'Malown' is said to come from 'luwn', *lodge*, *grumble* or *complain* or from 'ma'own', *dwelling*, *habitation* or *refuge*. The combination of these last two effectively enables 'ma'al' to be read within the word—'ma'al' meaning *to act unfaithfully or treacherously against God or man or a devoted thing*.

16 Yechiel Eckstein, 'Every End is a New Beginning', *Holy Land Moments Daily Devotional*, 25 May 2015

17 *'But I am afraid that just as Eve was deceived by the serpent's cunning, your minds may somehow be led astray from your sincere and pure devotion to Christ.'* (2 Corinthians 11:3 NIV)

18 There are so many great internet articles on blood covenant, you don't even have to go to a book to find out all about it. Just search. Salt covenant is a bit harder to track down. At the time of writing, I like the audio CD by John Sandford of *Elijah House*. However when it comes to threshold covenants and name covenants, it's trickier. There is some good material available on thresholds, but none of it goes into the long-term consequences of what happens when a covenant goes wrong—except for my books, *God's Pageantry* and *God's Pottery*. They not only deal with threshold covenants but with their intimate link to name covenants. *God's Poetry* is the only book currently I know of dedicated to name covenants and how they influence both your identity and your calling.

19 The dialogue between Mary Magdalene in the garden following Jesus' resurrection reflects the bridal sequence of the *Song of Songs*. Mary is the archetypal representative of the Bride of Christ: the first follower to witness to Him as Lord over death. Three times in the twentieth chapter of John's gospel, Mary wonders: 'Where is Jesus?'

John 20:2—'*So she came running to Simon Peter and the other disciple, the one Jesus loved, and said, "They have taken the Lord out of the tomb, and we don't know where they have put Him!"*'

John 20:13—'They [the angels] asked her, "Woman, why are you crying?" "They have taken my Lord away," she said, "and I don't know where they have put Him."'

John 20:15—' "Woman," He said, "why are you crying? Who is it you are looking for?" Thinking He was the gardener, she said, "Sir, if you have carried Him away, tell me where you have put Him, and I will get Him."'

In these verses, there are distant echoes of both:

Genesis 3:9—'But the Lord God called to the man, "Where are you?" 'and also Song of Songs 6:1–2—'"Where has your lover gone, most beautiful of women? Which way did your lover turn, that we may look for him with you?' 'My lover has gone down to his garden, to the beds of spices, to browse in the gardens and to gather lilies."'

20 Brian Simmons, Footnote 19:30, "It is finished, My Bride!" This is from the Aramaic word 'kalah,' a homonym with two meanings. It can mean "fulfilled (completed)," but is commonly used as the Aramaic (and Hebrew) word for "bride". Jesus finished the work of our salvation for his bride. The translation has combined both concepts. For a fascinating study of the Hebrew word used for "bride" and "finished," with its universe of meaning, see Strong's #3615, 3616, 3617,

3618, and 3634. Although the completed work of salvation was finished on the cross, He continues to work through His church today to extend the kingdom of God on the earth and glorify the Father through us. He continues to work in us to accomplish all that His cross and resurrection have purchased for us, His bride. His cross fulfilled and finished the prophecies of the Messiah's first coming to the earth. There was nothing written that was not fulfilled and now offered to His bride.

21   Kenneth Leech, *We Preach Christ Crucified*, Darton, Longman & Todd Ltd 2006.

22   The location where Simon had confessed Jesus was the Messiah and Jesus had given him the name 'Cephas' or 'Peter'.

23   The early Christian historian Eusebius says that it was reported that this woman came from Caesarea Philippi, where her house was to be seen. At the time, there were displayed some wonderful monuments of the benefits conferred upon her by Christ. At the door of her house was an statue of a woman in brass, set upon an high stone on her bended knees, and arms stretched out like a supplicant. Opposite her was a statue of a man, made of the same metal. The man was standing, clothed in a tunic, his hand was stretched out to the statue of the woman. At her feet upon the pillar, a strange plant grew. It reached up to the hem of the man's brass tunic and was said to be a remedy against all diseases. Eusebius says the statue was still to be seen in his times but Theophylact reported that in the days of the Roman emperor, Julian the apostate, it was broken into pieces.

24   *Silence in the Bible*, Paolo Torresan, Jewish Bible Quarterly, Vol. 31, No. 3, 2003

25   Yechiel Eckstein, 'More Precious than Pearls', *Holy Land Moments Daily Devotional*, 3 February 2016

www.ingramcontent.com/pod-product-compliance
Lightning Source LLC
Chambersburg PA
CBHW071023080526
44587CB00015B/2477